POINT REYES
VISIONS
GUIDEBOOK

Dana's Cell
640-1153

Where to go,

What to do,

★

in Point Reyes

National Seashore

&

its environs

D0949114

LICHEN & BAY TREES
Olema Valley

POINT REYES
VISIONS
GUIDEBOOK

Where to go,

What to do,

in Point Reyes National Seashore

&

its environs

PHOTOGRAPHS BY RICHARD P. BLAIR

TEXT BY KATHLEEN P. GOODWIN

COLOR & LIGHT EDITIONS
Inverness, California

POINT REYES HEADLANDS
From the Chimney Rock Trail

First Edition

ISBN 0-9671527-0-4 Clothbound
ISBN 0-9671527-2-0 Paperback

Printed in Singapore

Library of Congress Control Number: 2004092362

AEROMOTOR BLADES
Nicasio

LOOKING SOUTH FROM ARCH ROCK
The end of Bear Valley Trail

POINT REYES: A NATURAL SANCTUARY, A HUMAN HAVEN

Every time I set foot in Point Reyes National Seashore, I am awed to have access to a place so extraordinary. National parks like Point Reyes add a critical dimension to our lives. They provide a place to renew our spirit, learn lessons from the past, improve our health, and experience the essence of wildness.

In over 20 years of exploring Point Reyes, I have never been disappointed during my adventures. Each trip, whether to saunter on park trails, walk the beaches, or quietly sit in a magical spot to watch wildlife, has provided me with an indelible memory. Each encounter has inspired me to investigate new areas or return to see how this dynamic place changes over time.

As one of the top six most biologically rich areas in the United States, Point Reyes National Seashore is an American treasure—an incomparable coastal sanctuary. Because of the abundance of life, its forests and shores have provided a haven for humans for 5,000 years and continue to do so today.

Walk softly on the land as you explore this spectacular place. We all have a tremendous responsibility to help keep Point Reyes healthy so that this wild gift can be passed on to future generations.

Richard Blair and Kathleen Goodwin have incredible insight into the phenomenal resources of the park. Their detailed knowledge is manifested in Kathleen's writing and Richard's remarkable photographs.

Don L. Neubacher

Don Neubacher is currently superintendent of Point Reyes National Seashore. He previously worked at Glacier Bay National Park and at the Presidio of San Francisco. He is devoted to the preservation of wild places and works with the community of West Marin to protect its precious quality of life.

EEL GRASS & DOCK, WESTERN SHORE
Tomales Bay

TABLE OF CONTENTS

LIST OF PHOTOGRAPHS

These images are available as collectable prints. See page 78

TREES IN FOG
Inverness Ridge

INTRODUCTION

"The Peninsula is what we have and there is no more where it came from."
– David Brower

This little book will guide you to many amazing places and magical experiences. We are so lucky that Point Reyes National Seashore and its environs have been saved by the National Park Service and its allies, the fiercely protective citizens of West Marin and the Bay area. We welcome you! Our parks are for your enjoyment and to nurture your spirit. Our ranches provide your food plus habitat for wildlife. We are going to lead you to incredible places, some of which are very delicate and contain animals and birds which are barely holding on because their habitats are nearly gone. You, in return, must respect these places. Humbly clean up even other people's litter, and thus be open to the feeling of ownership of a common space which we all need. Slow down and look around.

We believe that people need to enjoy such a place. We know that parks breed nature activists. Since two million visitors come here each year, that can be a lot of votes that are pro-environment. If you like national parks, vote and encourage your friends to vote. When you're back home, revitalized by Point Reyes, work to make your own environment and community as healthy as possible.

When we plan a trip here, we think, where will it be nice today? What's the weather like, how much time do we have, what's going on in the natural world? Is the tide going out? We think about beauty, our comfort and safety, and about opportunity. We visualize what beautiful sights we might see and what animals could be around. Learning about the Point Reyes peninsula is the study of a lifetime. The more you see, discover and study, the greater pleasure you will feel being here.

Point Reyes juts into the sea so it has a marine climate. The weather is the same as being out in the Pacific Ocean. Once, on a clear day, we were walking on the beach near the Cliff House in San Francisco and were shocked to see how far west the Point Reyes headland appeared in the ocean. It looked like an island. The ocean water is quite cold (47-55 degrees) because of the circulation of the ocean currents. The coast is often foggy from the cold water condensing the moisture in the air. During the summer, the heat rising in the Central Valley draws the fog inland. By mid-morning the fog has usually burned off, and returns in the late afternoon.

The changeable nature of the weather brings a luminous quality to the landscape, a wonderful asset for a visual artist. The bishop pine and Douglas fir forests are hauntingly beautiful when shrouded in fog. During spring, the hills are an almost unreal green. I always think that spring has arrived when I see my first Douglas iris of the year. California poppies, lupine, yarrow, mustard and Indian paintbrush bloom all over. The discovery of a Mission Bell flower is a rare treat.

Point Reyes is part of the Pacific Plate and is on a part of the Earth's floating crust that is separate from the rest of North America. The land is moving north at the rate a fingernail grows (an average of an inch a year), and since the plates are joined by rock and mountains, the movement is jerky and occurs as earthquakes. Geologists have found this happens at approximately 80 year intervals.

However the connection of water and land is simpler to observe and enjoy. Beaches, for example, and rocky cliffs with pounding waves, isolated coves, sunny surfing and sunbathing spots.

The peninsula is a landscape that one has to experience. Walking on the trails and beaches, observing the birds, biking out to the coast, swimming in Tomales Bay. The important thing is to get out of the house, out of the car and to enjoy the natural world. Point Reyes National Seashore has 147 miles of trails and four backcountry campgrounds.

WHITE OR FALLOW DEER
Olema Valley
These animals are non-native deer that were introduced by a hunter.

Sightings of wild life are virtually guaranteed. The tule elk population has exploded since they were re-introduced to Tomales Point in 1978. The original 13 elk (2 males and 11 females) have been prolific. More than 450 elk roam in a territory that has been expanded beyond Tomales Point to include Limantour Beach and Drakes Bay.

The elephant seals are also flourishing. After an absence of more than 150 years, they returned in the 1970s. There are now several colonies. Their stay on these shores is cyclical: they are here in the winter (for the birth of the pups) and the spring (mating season). Bulls and cows travel separately the rest of the year, returning to Point Reyes at different times to molt.

Tomales Bay is one of the few places in Northern California where it is warm enough to swim in salty, ocean water. As the bay is long and shallow, the temperature of the water rises significantly during the summer. It is often possible to have an enjoyable swim as late in the season as November.

The Coast Miwok were the first known human inhabitants of Point Reyes. Over 100 sites where they lived have been found in the park. Some were seasonal, more like campsites, others were substantial villages where several hundred people may have lived. They helped Sir Francis Drake when he landed in 1579, at Drakes Bay (according

SURF EDDY AND CHIMNEY ROCK
Limantour Beach

to the latest evidence). Not long after that, the missionaries arrived and recruited the locals both as Christian converts and as workers.

The idyllic life of the Coast Miwoks, with its ample diet of deer, quail, wild lettuce, salmon, herring, oysters, nuts, berries and mussels, could not last after the white settlers arrived. Their enslavement

ELEPHANT MOUNTAIN SUNSET
Tomales Bay During El Nino
Photo: Kathleen P. Goodwin

by the missionaries, and the diseases the Indians caught at the missions played a large role in the demise of the Coast Miwok. Their traditional territory was parcelled off as land grants and ranches were established.

Olema, Bolinas, Inverness and Point Reyes were founded and the railway soon followed to what became Point Reyes Station. It was still a major journey from San Francisco, so the area never grew in a suburban kind of way. The Point Reyes National Seashore was created in 1962 but it took a petition, "Save Our Seashore," signed by half a million people to induce the US Congress in 1969 to provide sufficient money to acquire all its 53,000 acres.

Now it is ours to enjoy and protect.

ELEPHANT ROCK
Mc Clures Beach

THE SHORES OF TOMALES BAY

GNARLED TREE AT SHELL POINT
Tomales Bay

Tomales Bay is an extraordinary body of water formed by the San Andreas fault, where the western edge of the North American continent rubs against the easternmost edge of the Pacific Plate. Water flows in and out of the bay with the tides. The ocean outlet is the mighty Pacific nine miles to the north. Past the town of Inverness are several public beaches, with picturesque names like Children's Beach,

CLAYTON & JOE CAST THE NET
Tomales Bay

Chicken Ranch Beach and Teacher's Beach. Chicken Ranch Beach is the easiest to find, just before the road leaves Tomales Bay to go west. There is a short trail to the beach. Early in the morning, when the sun is rising across the protected waters of Tomales Bay, the western shore is lit by the sun. The water is often mirrorlike. You might see pelicans, egrets and herons sunning themselves. Dogs are allowed.

As Tomales Bay is shallow, long and narrow, it is eminently swimmable during the summer and fall when the water near the shore warms up. It is the most pristine bay on the US Pacific Coast. Fishermen catch mostly halibut, sturgeon, perch and herring here. Oysters and mussels also thrive. There is an old mercury mine in the watershed which is polluting the fish somewhat, so eat what you catch sparingly. The mercury does not affect the oysters, we've been told.

When the moon is full or new, great lengths of the shoreline are accessible at low tide. (Check a tide book). Then you can walk for miles, in and out of beautiful coves complete with sea caves, overhanging lichen on the trees, mussels and rock oysters on the rocks and seaweed-festooned logs on the sandy shores. Be sure to time your walk to return before the tide comes in and submerges your route.

THE WRECK OF THE POINT REYES
Inverness, Tomales Bay

MORNINGS

If it's raining, read the paper beside a fire or wood stove or stay in bed. Local bakeries offer excellent pastries, breads and coffee. The weekly newspaper, The Point Reyes Light, faithfully reports all upcoming community events and offers an interesting perspective on current issues. The daily New York Times is available locally. The Jack Mason Museum, which shares a space with the library in Inverness, often hosts historical exhibits.

SUNRISE AT WHITE GULCH
Tomales Bay

But if it's not too wet out and you're feeling energetic, go down to Tomales Bay at dawn and greet the morning light. You'll be rewarded with the magic of the place. Birds are active at sunrise, so listen for their songs. Kayaking, canoeing and rowing are best done early, before winds and waves pick up. Fog can be hanging in the valleys and when the sun rays strike it in the morning, it glows. Point Reyes beaches often are wonderful in the morning, when the cliffs are lit, and you are the only one there.

PICNICS

Tomales Bay State Park, north of Inverness, particularly Heart's Desire Beach, is a wonderful place for a picnic. The most secluded tables are on the hillside overlooking the beach.

Bear Valley and Drakes Beach also have picnic areas while on the southern end of Tomales Bay, at White House Pool, there are benches and a picnic table alongside Papermill Creek. Mount Vision, with its panoramic view of Tomales Bay and the Pacific Coast, is especially suited for romantic sunset dinners, although there are no formal picnic facilities.

PAPERMILL CREEK AT WHITE HOUSE POOL

PLACES TO WATCH THE SUNSET

A good rule of thumb on the west coast is to head for a beach at sunset. Limantour Beach often has spectacular sunsets, with the sand turning a golden brown while the cliffs light up with an orange and pink glow. At dusk, the sounds of the frogs in the wetlands resembles an orchestra.

The view west from Mount Vision toward the setting sun encompasses Drakes Estero, Chimney Rock, acres of farmlands, and miles of coastline. McClures Beach is another favorite spot to close the day. Take a flashlight so that you can safely wait until the light totally fades before heading back.

CHIMNEY ROCK & DRAKE'S ESTERO
from Mount Vision

MOONLIT MADNESS

MOONRISE OVER MARIN HEADLANDS
From Highway One

Full moons stir the soul. When the moon is full, it is lined up opposite the sun, causing very high and very low tides. These are called spring tides. The moon's effect on people is no less profound. It's time to walk the beaches or the trails, braving the mountain lions and frogs, to participate in primeval Point Reyes. Any of the trails mentioned in this book are good, but bring a flashlight for the fog, which can drift in at any time. Owls are hooting in the woods. The moon rises over Tomales Bay, so find a good perch to watch its progress from any of the beaches along the western shore. Listen for loons.

SURF BY MOONLIGHT
Great Beach

LIMANTOUR BEACH

Limantour Beach is a long expanse of coastline in Drakes Bay. On its southern end is Coast Camp, while its northern end is a sand spit which forms the border of Drakes Estero – a huge saltwater bay and marsh where oysters are grown. Thousands of birds roost in wetlands that parallel the beach. At dusk they wheel and turn in huge flocks, dividing into different patterns of perfect harmony. These wetlands offer an abundance of bird life in all seasons, so try to bring binoculars and a bird book.

A small herd of tule elk was moved from Pierce Point to the Limantour area in 1999 to expand their range. They are usually seen south of Limantour Beach in the hills alongside the Coast Camp trail.

Walk north to the mouth of Drakes Estero by turning right at the beach entrance or follow the old road, just before the beach, which skirts the estero part of the way, then go over the dunes to the end. This is a favorite haulout site of harbor seals. Sometimes, as many as eighty seals of all ages bask on the beach just above the tide line. Sit on the beach some distance away and watch them through binoculars,

LIMANTOUR BEACH
from Coast Camp

LIMANTOUR SPIT, ESTERO, AND CHIMNEY ROCK

as they are easily disturbed.

Because of these seals and the endangered snowy plover, dogs on leashes are only allowed south of the entrance to the beach.

Directions: From Highway One in Olema, turn left on Bear Valley Road, then left on Limantour Road. The road goes over Inverness Ridge; at the crest is the trailhead to Mt. Wittenberg and Sky Camp. Continue to the end of the road at the beach. The beach is a great walk north or south.

DRAKES BEACH

DRAKES BEACH FROM PETER BEHR OVERLOOK

Protected by the Point Reyes headlands, Drakes Beach usually has gentle surf. It is our favorite beach for wet-suit "boogie-boarding." The water is very cold all year. Even when the coast is engulfed in fog, this beach will often have sunshine.

Whales, particularly mothers with their calves, occasionally swim into the bay on their return migration from Baja up the coast to Alaska in the spring.

Sir Francis Drake is reputed to have landed at Drakes Bay and exclaimed that the cliffs reminded him of the "White cliffs of Dover." Pottery dating to 1579, the year Drake landed on the west coast, has been found on this beach.

A path leads up to the spectacular Peter Behr Overlook, named for the man who played a big part in preserving this area as a national park. Walk to the right (when facing the beach), until you see the narrow paved trail going steeply up a small hill.

During the winter, elephant seals establish colonies at the northern end of Drakes Beach. These are best seen from the Chimney Rock seal overlook.

MALE ELEPHANT SEAL IN REPOSE
Drakes Beach
Photo: Kathleen P. Goodwin

Directions from Inverness: Go north and west on Sir Francis Drake Boulevard in the direction of the Lighthouse. This will eventually bring you the side road to Drakes Beach (turn left at the sign).

BEACHES NORTH OF THE POINT

The Great Beach, north of the Point Reyes Lighthouse, extends eleven miles. The ocean here is wild and the currents strong, so keep an eye open for sneaker waves. The Great Beach comprises four beaches: South Beach, North Beach, Abbotts Lagoon and Kehoe Beach.

SILVER OCEAN, GREAT BEACH AND POINT REYES HEADLANDS
From the hills behind Kehoe Beach

ABBOTTS LAGOON

A 1.5 mile walk through coastal scrub, across an isthmus between two lagoons, and over sand dunes brings you to this wide expansive ocean beach. From here, one can walk two miles north to Kehoe Beach while a three mile hike south will end at North Beach. These are unusual beach walks and are good choices if you want to experience solitude.

The lagoons attract large numbers of migrating shorebirds in the fall followed by the wintering ducks. Occasionally peregrine falcons are seen preying on the birds. The sand dunes behind the beach are home to the endangered snowy plover. The eggs and young of this ground-nesting bird are easily destroyed. Be especially careful in this area during their nesting season, early June through mid-September.

At sunset, Abbotts lagoon often shimmers in golden light.

ABBOTTS LAGOON

KEHOE BEACH

The short trail to Kehoe Beach follows a stream along a marsh then transverses a sand dune. At the beach the meandering stream meets the sea. To the north, high cliffs border the beach. A reverse fault placed sandstone against granite, creating a dramatic colorful juxtaposition of rocks reminiscent of southwestern desert canyon walls. Cows look down from the heights. One can walk south along the beach for about 11 miles, and a group can arrange a car shuttle.

Try hiking up the hills behind the beach. As one ascends, the view south reveals undulating hills, the Great Beach, and flashes from the lighthouse. Far north is Bodega Head. Wildflowers, particularly lupine and California poppy, abound in the spring.

Dogs with leashes are allowed on Kehoe beach.

MC CLURES BEACH

A short, steep, downhill hike brings you to this small but exciting cove with intense surf. On the southern part of the beach is a narrow passage to an adjacent beach that can only be safely accessed during the outgoing low tide. Between the beaches is a dramatic rock pushing its way out to sea. From its peak are panoramic views of the coast. It is a great place to photograph and paint. Care must be taken here – several people have been swept off its edge into the ocean by unexpectedly big waves. This is for experienced ocean-aware climbers only, not kids! A little further out to sea is a small, rocky island, a favorite perch of pelicans, cormorants and gulls.

ROCK SPIRE AND GULL
Cove south of Mc Clures Beach

MC CLURES BEACH

Directions: The trailhead is down the road from Pierce Point Ranch, which has been lovingly restored as a showcase of farm architecture in Northern California. Many elk are often grazing in the area.

THE POINT REYES LIGHTHOUSE

THE POINT REYES LIGHTHOUSE ON A BLUSTERY DAY

The Point Reyes Lighthouse was built in 1870 after more than 60 shipwrecks had occurred at the point. It was forged from iron plate and bolted into solid rock in the cliff. The lantern room contains a Fresnel lens, 7'10" high, which weighs three tons. Manufactured in Paris, it was ingeniously designed so that the thousand hand-ground prisms in the lens could focus the weak light of oil lamps into 24 powerful rays. These rays could be seen up to 30 miles out to sea. The first-order Fresnel lens, so called because it is the largest lens of its type, is no longer operational on a daily basis. Occasionally it is switched on for public viewing and one sees the lens slowly turning.

The lighthouse is reached by walking down 308 steps. During high winds the lighthouse is closed, but the observation deck at the top of the steps remains open.

Whale-watching is a popular activity at the Lighthouse. Gray whales migrate from Alaska down to Baja starting in November. The whales both mate and give birth in the warm shallow waters of Scammon's Lagoon and Magdalena Bay on Baja's Pacific coast, then return to Alaska starting in February.

Directions: The Lighthouse is at the end of Sir Drakes Drake Blvd. Because of the amount of traffic, visitors may be asked to park their cars at South Beach or Drakes Beach and take a Park Service shuttle bus.

THE POINT REYES LIGHTHOUSE LIT AT DUSK

TIDEPOOLING

The best tidepooling in this area is at Duxbury Reef and Agate Beach in Bolinas. Extensive tidepools are just a few minutes' stroll from the entrances to these beaches.

The most rewarding time to tidepool is, of course, at low tide, when starfish and sea anemones can be seen. Minus tides at any of these beaches are the best of all. Classes given by the College of Marin and walks with marine scientists reveal a strange world that seems populated with creatures that defy belief.

SEA ANEMONE
Cove south of Mc Clures Beach

STARFISH

PLYING THE WATERS

Kayaking and canoeing are popular on Tomales Bay. The coves on both sides of the bay lend themselves to exploration. The wind often increases dramatically toward late morning and in the afternoon so plan to be flexible, giving weather conditions the highest priority. Drakes Estero is another outstanding area for human-powered crafts. Kayaks are available to rent locally. Jet skis are banned!

Windsurfers are sometimes seen skimming the waves at Limantour Beach or offshore along Tomales Bay. They often find themselves challenged in the heavy winds funneling through the bay.

KAYAKER

FIRE ROAD TR/
Inverness Ridge near Sky Ca

HIKING TRAILS IN THE POINT REYES AREA

There is great variety to the trail hikes here. Some are easy strolls, others could be challenging for an athlete. The wind and fog, which are almost ever present here, dictate what you need to wear and where to go. If the coast is clear, try Chimney Rock, Tomales Point or Mt. Tamalpais. In strong northwesterly winds we suggest Bear Valley, or along Tomales Bay. If there's a wild storm, dress with fleece and Gore-Tex, and have fun, but beware of dangers like falling trees and hypothermia. Poison oak and nettles abound and both cause severe rashes from the leaves. If you are stuck in brush, keep your hands in your pockets and your pant legs in your socks. Bring water, lunch, binoculars, map, matches, and a few Band Aids for blisters if they develop. A small flashlight in the pack is a good idea in case you come back late. "Be prepared," as the Scouts remind us. Remember: this place is so beautiful that the effort you make to hike here will be repaid in sights that you'll cherish for a lifetime.

FOG FROM MOUNT VISION

ELEPHANT MOUNTAIN
from Bolinas Ridge Trail

OLEMA TO MOUNT TAMALPAIS VIA THE BOLINAS RIDGE
(or vice-versa)

The Bolinas Ridge Trail runs for 11 miles from Mount Tamalpais to Sir Francis Drake Boulevard, about a mile east of Olema. There are many ways to access the trail. The simplest is to start at the trailhead on Sir Francis Drake Blvd. From here you can walk part or all of the way to Mt. Tamalpais. En route you will pass trails that connect to Samuel P. Taylor State Park. Even on a short walk, you immediately see expansive panoramas and experience a feeling of wide open space. The sight and sounds of the road are soon left behind.

The other end of the trail begins on Mount Tamalpais at the junction of the Bolinas-Fairfax Road and Ridgecrest Boulevard. It heads north over several steep knolls, followed by a long downhill stretch through a redwood forest. Several miles later the trail launches into the wild blue yonder of open ridge grassland, with views of Tomales

Bay, Inverness Ridge, Bolinas Lagoon, Elephant Mountain and Mount Barnabe. The trail is open to bicyclists. Dogs are also allowed.

If two cars are available, a one-way hike is possible. Leave one car at the trailhead at Olema Hill, where Sir Francis Drake Blvd. crests, and drive to the junction of Ridgecrest Road and Bolinas–Fairfax Road, high on Mt. Tamalpais, to start the hike. The 11 miles is mostly downhill but give yourselves plenty of time. At the end of the trail, return and pick up the first car. It is worth the effort to hike or bike this great trail. This is a full-day hike. (Most hikers walk at about 2 miles per hour plus an hour added for each thousand feet gained in elevation.)

BOLINAS RIDGE
from Highway One

AT BEAR VALLEY

The Bear Valley Visitors' Center, situated between Olema and Inverness, is a major source of information, advice and publications about Point Reyes National Seashore. It has exhibits on the animals, plants, geology and history of the park. A slide show that runs frequently gives an overview of the park, and a constantly changing art exhibit contributes creative interpretations of West Marin.

A spot where a cow reputedly fell into a crack in the earth during the famous 1906 San Francisco earthquake can be seen on the Earthquake Trail that starts near the visitors' center. The epicenter of the earthquake lies on this scenic trail and a break in a fence graphically shows the 16 feet of movement of the Pacific plate. The asphalt path is wheel chair accessible. The farmer was suspected of faking the cow story, by the way.

If you want a longer, more challenging hike, choose the Bear Valley Trail off the large parking lot beyond the visitors' center. The four-mile path winds its way through a lush forest along a stream, past Divide Meadow, and ends at Arch Rock, a promontory that juts out to sea, giving a spectacular view up and down the coast (see the frontispiece). Divide Meadow, 1.5 miles along the path, was formerly the site of a hunting lodge where Teddy Roosevelt once hunted. It is now a favorite spot for picnics; grazing deer are often seen there. The trail is open to equestrians and bicyclists as well. Its hard dirt surface makes it suitable for wheelchairs and strollers almost all the way to the coast.

BEAR VALLEY CREEK

TIDELINE, ARCH ROCK
Bear Valley Trail
Photo: Kathleen P. Goodwin

TREES AT DIVIDE MEADOW
Bear Valley Trail

POINT REYES HEADLANDS & DRAKES BAY
View from Chimney Rock Trail

CHIMNEY ROCK TRAIL

With its magnificent spring wildflowers, dramatic landscapes and ocean views, the trail to Chimney Rock is one of the finest short hikes in the United States.

The trail follows the ridge and goes to the aptly named rock formation at the southern tip of the Point Reyes headlands. After half a mile and atop a hill, a side trail branching off to the west takes you to a spectacular panorama of the cliffs, Pacific Ocean and Drakes Bay. On the isolated beaches between Chimney Rock and the Lighthouse to the west, many seals, sea lions and elephant seals lie 'hauled out'. The sandy shore offers them a place to rest, provides a respite from the sharks, and allows the pinnipeds to warm themselves, mate and raise pups in season. The park service has closed this beach to let these wild creatures live undisturbed. In winter, the overlooks along the Chimney Rock trail offer prime whale watching, particularly during February and March, when the gray whale mothers and their calves travel close to the shore as they return from Baja, Mexico on their way to Alaska.

The hike to Chimney Rock and back is less than two miles with just one short, steep incline. On Drakes Bay you will see the historic lifesaving station and an active commercial fishing dock We would rate this hike as moderately easy while the views gained are second to none.

LUPINE AND LICHEN
Chimney Rock Trail in Spring

Directions: Take the road towards the Point Reyes Lighthouse; a few miles past the turnoff to Drakes Beach, you'll see a fork on the left to Chimney Rock. The narrow road leads to the trailhead parking.

CLIMBING MOUNT WITTENBERG

At 1407 feet, Mount Wittenberg is the highest point in the Point Reyes National Seashore. It can be approached from the Bear Valley Trail or via an easier hike that starts at the Sky Trailhead off Limantour Road. Either way is an energetic hike of about five miles round trip but the reward is a great view of the coast line and the Farallon Islands. At the summit, there is a filtered view, through the Douglas fir trees, of Mount Tamalpais, Elephant (or Black) Mountain and Twin Peaks.

Though at times a little steep, the path is fairly smooth which makes Mount Wittenberg a good place to watch the sunset. Walk back in the moonlight or with the aid of a flashlight. Because many trails lead to Mount Wittenberg it is easy to climb it one way and return by a different trail via Bear Valley, thus being in the lush, stream habitat as well as the

OAK TREE BRANCHES ARCHING OVER PATH
Sky Trail From Limantour Road

BEACH GRASSES AND DUNES
Limantour Beach

BEACH WALKING

The place most people hike in Point Reyes National Seashore is, naturally, along the many miles of beaches. The longest beach in the park is the Great Beach, which is 10 miles from the cliffs near the lighthouse to the end of Kehoe Beach. The ocean here is cold, normally about 50 degrees, so the winds and fog off the ocean are cold. The best clothing is fleece with a windproof layer. Some days are bikini weather, especially in the fall. Some people like hiking boots, others prefer sandals or even walking barefoot. There is always a lot to see. Occasionally curious marine mammals will follow you. You can even see whales in season (December to March). One finds lots of strange stuff people have thrown in the ocean and fishing floats. It's important to know the tides so you don't get stranded. Watch the surf too!!

HIKE TO SUNSET BEACH

Off the beaten track, Sunset Beach is aptly named. From its shores on a clear day you can see the setting sun light up the entrance to Drakes Estero. With Chimney Rock and the Farallon Islands both visible in the distance, this spot can be a stunning end to the day.

The hike to Sunset Beach is about 4 miles each way. Begin at the Estero trailhead, just past the turn off to Mount Vision on Sir Francis Drake Boulevard. The path first winds through pastureland, passes through a Monterey pine forest, and then reaches a wooden bridge. This is a good spot for birdwatching and could make an enjoyable destination. If your goal is Sunset Beach however, continue on the trail as it climbs along the estero and up and down three canyons (about 2.5 miles) until you reach the signpost to Sunset Beach, 1.5 miles ahead. At the beach, hundreds of shorebirds forage along the shoreline, seals swim in the estero and lie hauled out at the end of Limantour Spit. If you look carefully, you may find whale bone fossils on the shore and scallop fossils embedded in the rocks.

The hike back will take more than an hour, so should you want to watch the sunset, remember to take a flashlight.

SUNSET BEACH

TOMALES POINT TRAIL

PIERCE POINT RANCH
Northern end of the Pierce Point Road

Of all the hikes in West Marin, the trail to Tomales Point is the one where you will almost always see wildlife. This area of the park, at the far end of Pierce Point Road, is home to six herds of tule elk. On a recent walk to the point, we saw three herds of tule elk, a long-tailed weasel, a bobtail rabbit, a vole, two deer, vultures, pelicans, cormorants, sea gulls, sea lion, and a great egret.

The trail begins at the restored buildings of the Pierce Point Ranch, one of the original dairy farms in the area and certainly worth a visit. It continues up and down grass-covered hills for almost five miles until Tomales Point is reached. Here at the confluence of Tomales Bay and the Pacific, the land seems to slide into the ocean. On the western side of the bay are deeply eroded canyons with layers of different-colored sand reminiscent of Death Valley. Toward Tomales Bay you will see Hog Island and idyllic beaches along the bay shoreline. Across the bay is Tom's Point where oysters, clams and abalone are farmed. South along the ocean is McClures Rock, then the Great Beach stretching away to the Point Reyes Headlands.

In the spring, the path is lined with wild yellow, white, and pale lilac radish. Yellow lupine bushes with their sweet perfume cover the ridge top, interspersed with wild hemlock, yellow mustard plants, California poppies, cockle burrs and wild yarrow. You might be lucky and see a newly born elk fawn still sporting spots.

ELK AND PACIFIC OCEAN
From Tomales Point Trail

SAMUEL P. TAYLOR STATE PARK

The main route to West Marin, Sir Francis Drake Boulevard, follows the lush Papermill Creek through the heart of Samuel P. Taylor State Park. The park encompasses redwood canyons, riparian habitat, Mount Barnabe with its wonderful views and other grassy coastal ridges.

In the nineteenth century Samuel Taylor, a former gold prospector, ran a water-powered mill a few miles from present day Lagunitas to produce paper. Like an early recycler, he made paper from rags his men collected in San Francisco and coastal towns. Piles of trouser buttons have been found by the creek! In 1870, Taylor built a resort

PAPERMILL CREEK IN DAPPLED SUN
Samuel P. Taylor State Park

hotel and campground next to his paper mill and established one of California's first vacation retreats to offer outdoor camping. In 1946 it became a state park.

TRAIL AT HORSE CAMP
Devils Gulch

Lagunitas and San Geronimo creeks both flow through the park. They join at Shafter Bridge, beyond the town of Lagunitas, to form a single creek, Papermill Creek, which eventually empties into Tomales Bay. Papermill Creek often overflows its banks in very wet years.

The main trail that runs through the park, from the campground to the bridge at Tocaloma, was originally part of the train system that connected Point Reyes to Larkspur. Now it is a wonderfully graded path, covered part of the way with asphalt, eminently suitable for wheelchairs, baby carriages and bicycles. It follows a green corridor of redwood, bay and laurel trees and is a rich riparian habitat.

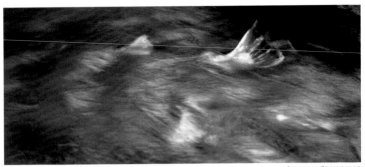

Both coho salmon and steelhead spawn in the streams in Samuel P. Taylor State Park. The annual salmon run dropped down to a handful of fish, but with the help of conservationists who have restored streambeds and repaired fishing ladders, the numbers of spawning fish are increasing.

Each year researchers at the Point Reyes National Seashore conduct salmon counts to see how the salmon are surviving in West Marin. With the help of volunteers, they count the number of female and male salmon, live or dead, and the number of nests, called redds, built by the females to hold their eggs.

CLIFFS AT HEART'S DESIRE BEACH
Tomales Bay State Park

TOMALES BAY STATE PARK

Encompassing 2,000 acres, Tomales Bay State Park includes some of the most beautiful beaches and coves on Tomales Bay, a stunning picnic area, and even campsites for hikers and bicyclists. Heart's Desire Beach is shaped like a horseshoe, with a large lawn area in the middle. This is a perfect park for families with young children. It has picnic tables, bathrooms, and cold showers. A half-mile nature walk trail to the north ends at Indian Beach, where two replicas of Miwok shelters of redwood bark (known as kotcas) have been constructed. A half mile hike south of Heart's Desire Beach leads to Pebble Beach. The trail climbs and descends through forest to Shell Beach.

Hand-carried boats may put into Tomales Bay at Heart's Desire Beach which has a parking area very close to the water and beach.

The park has other sections across Tomales Bay on the east shore, notably Millerton Point, three miles north of Point Reyes Station which has great hiking and birdwatching. Maps of the complete park are found on the web at www.parks.ca.gov.

BIKING & MOUNTAIN BIKING

Marin County is the birthplace of the mountain bike, created when people combined the fat tires used on cruisers with the gearing of road bikes. Now popular all over the world, mountain bikes are amazingly well suited to explore our local terrain.

West Marin is a mecca for cyclists. Every weekend hundreds of bicyclists, many riding with clubs, are all over West Marin roads. Many have stunning bikes, and if you are a cycling aficionado, you'll be fascinated by the riders and their gear.

The roads here are hilly, two lanes and offer extraordinary scenic rewards. Unfortunately, the same beauty also attracts people who love to drive the same two-lane roads at high speeds in both cars and motor cycles. Some drivers are rigid, don't slow down or pass too

SPALETTA DAIRY AND POINT REYES HEADLANDS
On the Road to the Lighthouse

close to the bicyclist. When you bicycle on the road, ride single file and stay on the right! Wear bright colors and have lights for twilight riding. Our solution is to take our bike trips during the week when traffic is light. We also choose less travelled roads. Plan your trip with a road map (and a topo map), keeping your own ability in mind. Fun is the goal!

THE SAMUEL P. TAYLOR BIKE TRAIL

Samuel P. Taylor State Park has a very easy bike trail because it is built on the old railroad grade that ran through the redwood canyon of Papermill Creek. The trail goes though redwoods, grasslands and mixed forest along a beautiful creek. Go to the park entrance on Sir Francis Drake Blvd. about 4 miles east of Olema and the rangers will direct you to the trail or start in Tocaloma where parking is free.

MOUNTAIN BIKING ON INVERNESS RIDGE
Trail to Mount Vision

BEAR VALLEY TRAIL

This trail, also popular with hikers, is described fully in the hiking section. The trail runs alongside a stream lined with lush ferns, bay trees, alders and Douglas fir. It climbs to Divide Meadow, about 400 feet of elevation gain over a mile and a half. Most people can make it to the top but some walk their bikes the last two hundred yards. The trail descends for about another mile and a half and then you reach a bike rack about a mile from the ocean. Bikes are not allowed any further, so bring a bike lock and walk the rest of the way to Arch Rock.

BOLINAS RIDGE TRAIL

An exciting mountain bike ride, this trail follows the ridge from near the top of Mount Tamalpais all the way to Olema. Our favorite method is to start from the top of the Bolinas-Fairfax road on Mount Tam and ride downhill to Olema, where we leave a second car. Strong riders can do it as a loop, taking Highway One from Olema to Bolinas. The road from Bolinas to the beginning of the trail atop the ridge was designed for horse-drawn stagecoaches and is moderately graded; it is uphill but not too difficult to ride. The ridge is knobby; both ways have uphill sections, but it is much easier to go north than south.

FIVE BROOKS TO WILDCAT BEACH

A *really* hard ride is the Five Brooks to Wildcat Beach ride in the National Seashore. The trailhead is five miles south of Point Reyes off Highway One. You ride up the east side of Inverness Ridge on an old farm road, which is well graded for mountain bikes. The ridge takes you through a lush forest with lichen on the trees and views across Olema Valley. Firtop, a tree-covered summit at 1300 feet above sea level, is the highest point of the ride. Then the trail descends sharply to the ocean, where there's a great beach and campground to explore.

Alamere Falls, a seasonal waterfall on the beach, is within walking distance from the end of the bike trail. The ride back is so steep that you'll have to walk the bike up the last section unless you are a really strong athlete.

ALAMERE FALLS
Near Wildcat Beach

OYSTERS

Oysters are one of the joys to be experienced while visiting West Marin. Not only can they be eaten here at the source, but their habitat can be observed and enjoyed. The Johnson Oyster Company on Drakes Estero makes an interesting destination Their oyster beds can also be observed at low tide from the Estero Trail.

There are three companies farming oysters in Tomales Bay, Hog Island Oyster Company, Point Reyes Oyster Company and Tomales Bay Oyster Company. Native to Tomales Bay is the Olympia oyster or *ostrea lurida*. Popular in the 1800s when the oysters in San Francisco Bay were eaten almost to extinction, the Olympia is now not usually considered commercially viable as it is both small and slow growing. Pacific, kumamoto, Atlantic and euroflat oysters are farmed in West Marin.

OYSTERMAN AT JOHNSON'S OYSTERS
Drakes Estero, Pt. Reyes National Seashore

CRAB AND OTHER LOCAL DELICACIES

Dungeness crab is another treat. In a good year much crab is brought to E Ranch by George Nunes, the farmer who runs the fish dock at Chimney Rock. There it is cooked in large vats of boiling water or sold live for those who want to experience the freshest crab by cooking it themselves just before eating. Mussels and clams are bounteous too. Abalone divers often reach the limit of their allowed catch on these shores. Our personal seafood favorite, sea urchin (known in sushi circles as *uni*), is abundant. Once you have tasted really fresh *uni*, it is hard to order it at a sushi bar.

SUN AND FOG, HOG ISLAND AND PIGLET
Tomales Bay

THE FISH STORY

One of the most productive areas of the Pacific Ocean is the Cordell Bank near the Farallon Islands, 22 miles west of the Point Reyes Lighthouse. It was discovered in 1853 by George Davidson of the U.S. Coast Survey while returning from a mapping expedition on California's north coast. The Cordell Bank, which is on the continental shelf, is an undersea island, 4.5 miles wide and 9.5 miles long. It is bathed by the upwelling of nutrient-rich water from the deep ocean. The base of the bank is at a depth of about 400 feet. It is part of the Cordell Bank National Marine Sanctuary, which protects 526 square miles off the coast.

FISHING IN BOLINAS

The sanctuary is an important feeding ground for the endangered blue and humpback whales that travel from their breeding areas in Mexico and Central America to feed on the abundant krill and schooling fish near the bank. In late summer, breaching humpbacks are seen frequently. Pacific white-sided dolphins, California sea lions, elephant seals, northern fur seals, and Steller sea lions are also attracted by the food resources. Halibut, perch, sturgeon, salmon, bass, thresher shark and rock cod are also common. Freshly caught fish are brought by local fishermen to the fish dock at Chimney Rock in Drakes Bay.

SALMON BOATS, OUTGOING TIDE
Bolinas Lagoon Dock

ANIMALS OF THE POINT REYES PENINSULA

HARBOUR SEAL PUP
Drakes Beach

MALE ELEPHANT SEAL
Great Beach

COYOTE
Tomales Point

MULE DEER
Tomales Point

GREAT EGRET
Rodeo Beach

MOUNTAIN LION
Point Reyes National Seashore

ELK
Tomales Point

RABBIT
Limantour Beach

BACKPACKING CAMPS IN THE SEASHORE

Campgrounds are open all year for backpackers or bicyclists. No dogs, horses or pack animals are allowed. Permits are needed.

Coast Camp is nestled in a small coastal valley with easy access to the beach and tidepools. The shortest hike to the camp is 1.8 miles along an almost flat trail from the Hostel off Limantour Road.

Glen Camp is a quiet and secluded camp deep within a Douglas fir forest. The shortest hike to the camp is a moderate 4.6 miles by foot or bicycle from Bear Valley. It is a 2.5 mile strenuous hike from there to the beach.

Sky Camp lies on the western slope of Mt. Wittenberg overlooking the Pacific Ocean. In clear weather, it has wonderful ocean views. The shortest hike to the camp is 1.3 miles on foot or bicycle from the trailhead at Limantour Road. It is a 4.5 mile moderately strenuous to hike to the beach.

Wildcat Camp is located on the coast near the southern end of the Seashore. The shortest hiking route is a moderate 5.5 mile hike along the Coast Trail from Palomarin. The only biking route is 6.7 miles from Five Brooks on the strenuous Stewart Trail. The beach and Alamere Falls are a short walk from camp.

GOOD DOGGIE!

DOGS IN THE WILDS OF WEST MARIN

The Point Reyes area is receptive to dogs but you should be aware that this natural place is home to rare creatures that need protection from your dog.

Access to certain beaches is restricted when the elephant seals are here and during the snowy plover nesting season.

Elephant seals congregate on South Beach from December through April to mate and to give birth – both people and dogs are disruptive. Occasionally other areas are closed when the seals find new territories for their reproduction.

An endangered bird, the snowy plover, makes its nest in the beach sand. Dogs find the nests so they are not allowed on the Great Beach between North Beach and Kehoe Beach from May through September.

Dogs are welcome at these five beaches the rest of the year.

Kehoe Beach
Limantour Beach - south of the parking lot
North Beach
South Beach
Chicken Ranch Beach on Tomales Bay (all year)

Papermill Creek in Samuel Taylor State Park is good for long walks. The Bolinas Ridge trail is also a great place to take your dog. They are allowed at the Bear Valley picnic area too. Marin Open Space district also allows dogs.

Leashes are required on all trails and beaches.

Call the park for specifics at 415 464-5100.

This book was written and designed by Kathleen Goodwin and Richard Blair. It was edited by Nancy Adess, and John Dell'Osso, and inspired by the food at Manka's Inverness Lodge. The photographs are by Richard Blair unless they are captioned K.P. Goodwin. We are the artists responsible for *Point Reyes Visions*, a 192-page color artisan book which is available locally.

Our studio and home is atop Inverness ridge on Drakes View Drive where many photographs and paintings are on view. It is open by appointment. Prints are printed to the highest technical and archival standards. The photographic images in the *Guide* can also be ordered by phone or through the website, pointreyesvisions.com, which offers even more information on Point Reyes National Seashore. It contains over 300 pages of detailed information about the park and has weather links, downloadable maps, and is a valuable companion to this book. When we have **shows** and teach **workshops**, information is posted online. You can also sign up to receive our *Newsletter* via email at rk@pointreyesvisions.com Gallery information is on our website too. We hope to see you on the trails!

Richard Blair & Kathleen Goodwin

371 Drakes View Drive
Inverness Park, CA 94937
415 663-1615

www.pointreyesvisions.com

COW CONTEMPLATING THE VOID
Nicasio